T0154771

Spit

Spit

POEMS BY **DANIEL LASSELL**

WHEELBARROW BOOKS ▪ *East Lansing, Michigan*

Copyright © 2021 by Daniel Lassell

⊗ The paper used in this publication meets the minimum requirements of ANSI/NISO Z39.48-1992 (R 1997) (Permanence of Paper).

Wheelbarrow Books
Michigan State University Press
East Lansing, Michigan 48823-5245

Michigan State University Press
East Lansing, Michigan 48823-5245

Library of Congress Control Number: 2020944439
ISBN 978-1-61186-396-3 (paper)
ISBN 978-1-60917-669-3 (PDF)
ISBN 978-1-62895-429-6 (ePub)
ISBN 978-1-62896-430-1 (Kindle)

Book design by Charlie Sharp, Sharp Des!gns, East Lansing, MI
Cover design by Erin Kirk
Cover art by Erin Kirk, based on *Llama*, by tomas ondrejka, Adobe Stock

g **green** Michigan State University Press is a member of the Green Press
press Initiative and is committed to developing and encouraging
ecologically responsible publishing practices. For more information about the
Green Press Initiative and the use of recycled paper in book publishing, please
visit *www.greenpressinitiative.org.*

Visit Michigan State University Press at *www.msupress.org*

With the publication of Daniel Lassell's collection of poems, *Spit*, the Residential College in the Arts and Humanities (RCAH) Center for Poetry at Michigan State University offers its eighth book in our Wheelbarrow Books Poetry Series. Clearly, we pay homage to William Carlos Williams and his iconic poem, "The Red Wheelbarrow." Readers will remember the poem begins "so much depends upon . . ." that red wheelbarrow. While "The Red Wheelbarrow" is not necessarily a farm poem, British and American literature are full of poems about the farm, animals on a farm, life on the farm, from the poems of Thomas Hardy and Edward Thomas to Paul Laurence Dunbar, John Ashbery, and perhaps the most famous contemporary poem by James Wright, "Lying in a Hammock on William Duffy's Farm in Pine Island, Minnesota." The farm is the vehicle for encountering truths. Daniel Lassell's *Spit* begins on a llama farm with the castration of a llama named James and John Sons of Thunder and concludes with the narrator reflecting on the past, the selling of the llama farm, the pain that comes with the locked door, the turning off of the lights. "End of the Llamas" includes the following section:

I am no longer farmer

unnamed

unnamed

\\

llamas return again to my windows
and I follow them

O what deep   eternal bucket
I might lean into

brimming   touched by tongues
          no

wake up   wake up

the llamas are gone

maybe my body is now the farm
a housing   where now I

carry them
       carry them

Spit (who wouldn't take a book with this title down off the shelf to see what's inside?) is part family story, part farm story, part coming-of-age story. It's a story mixing humor and violence, interior and exterior landscapes, faith and despair. Life is hard and often ends in loss. But there is no sentimentality here, just the cold eye of observation and the softer edges of memory. There is healing, ultimately, a blessing.

One might ask, why in this world of COVID-19, Black Lives Matter, children in cages at our border, historic unemployment, and economic despair, why do we need a book of poems about llamas? This is no *Llama Llama Red Pajama*, no bedtime story for children. We need poems about llamas because they are peculiar to one person's experience, to the world for him, on which so much depends. We read poems to understand how ordinary people, like ourselves, deal with ordinary emotions like joy and love, grief and loss. From the pen of a skilled poet, we can learn just as much by encountering a llama as we can a riot in the streets. It's a matter of perspective, what the poet and the reader bring to the page.

As our number of Wheelbarrow Books increases, we hope that our audience increases also. Help us spread the word. In the beginning was the word, and the word became the poem. So much depends upon the collaboration of reader, writer, and poem, the intimate ways we come to know one another. So much depends upon this relationship.

—ANITA SKEEN, *Wheelbarrow Books Series Editor*

f you told me I'd be choosing a book about llamas for the Wheelbarrow Books poetry prize, I'm not sure I would have believed you. Particularly in these radically difficult and, hopefully, radically visionary times. It seems worth saying in this citation that I write this in a time where we are in a global pandemic. Where many of us have only left our house in the last three months in order to protest the ceaseless brutalities and injustices imposed upon Black people in this country. It is, in short, a time when I did not know if poems were the thing I either wanted or needed. A time when being sent a pile of very fine manuscripts of poems was not something I knew if I was up to "judging."

Yes, I think it's worth saying the time we're in, when these poems came to me. As cases of COVID-19 rose and rose here in North Carolina and as activists risked their lives in so many ways to be out protesting and fighting for a more just and equitable world, I kept coming back to my house and rereading Daniel Lassell's *Spit*. A book, ostensibly, about a childhood and young life farming llamas! A book filled with a seemingly tight focus that kept reminding me of all the complexities and harms and beauties of the larger world outside. A book about agrarian life that touches on faith, violence, the tick-borne illnesses that seem to be bringing so many bodies low, in this era where all of our bodies are in danger. It is a book that takes account of itself and where the agrarian life is a lens but never a veil, never an idyll. Life is hard in these poems. And the body keeps persevering as it also attempts to see the possibility of another way of being.

There are so many things we need right now. Who knows what the world will even look like when this book comes out? And who knows what it will look like if you are reading this book many years from now? This book, to me, seems timeless and utterly present in its desire, through the hard work of formal rigor and dreaming, to look deeply at the damaged and often beautiful world as a means of making something new.

—GABRIELLE CALVOCORESSI

Contents

For my family, near and far

I.

The Llama Named James and John Sons of Thunder

Mom named him that because she's into the Bible. When you live on a farm, every animal receives a name. This is what a Christian household looks like. So, we called that llama *James and John Sons of Thunder*. Two names in one llama, the Trinity in a lesser form. A symbol for expansive personhood. But my brothers and I joked it referred to his testicles: those *sons* of Thunder. Those sons who bulged in summer heat, who shriveled on crisp mornings. Those sons who drove him to straddle the fence line in pursuit of females. And led to his castration. That day the vet cut them out, scalpeling the sack and loosening them from their hold, my brothers and I stood with sunken shoulders, witnessing a funeral. Two little orbs emerged, cupped from the heat, white like a molded sphere of dried candle wax. I watched them disappear into the woods. (Did you know they bounce?) The llama's head voiced nothing, tongue limp in the barn floor dust. Now he's just called *Thunder*.

Laws of Motion

A surface to break
    a surface.

        In this bush hog,
brush

    into splinter.

Pollen into any nostril.

    My family crops a map from

elbowed

        stems,

     time: a descending fist.

      It is summer.

      Sopping,
      hazy
      Kentucky.

Smaller creatures,
    accustomed to silence,

riffle through the noise for
          safety.

    Even safety
equals a room

in motion.

Instant death—is it

a better death?

Like spittle, their blood

feathers

when forced open.

What becomes wind

when the dead
live in it?

What becomes a farm

when by blade,

an emptiness
is called *clean*,

godly?

The Wolves Next Door

I would hear them
from my family's porch,
their howling like humidity.

During the day, if I biked
to where our gravel driveway
gnawed the county road,

I would find our bearded neighbor,
proud of his purchase,
shouldering bags of dog food.

Mom shook her head,
You can't cage fate.
And fate unraveled a wildness,

snouts turning beneath wire
to sun-flecked woods.
The wolves rolled about,

as if clenched upon withers
they could release a synapse,
an ancient blood,

send their nostrils suddenly back
to when their relatives
deemed brittle the bones

       of elk,
             rabbit,
     bison.

They traded throaty bellows,
dug wide the earth,
and stamped apart

the steeples of ant mounds.
Such violence in the
darkness and light of selfhood.

To subdue fear, I thought,
could be the same as ruffling
the ears of danger.

So, I jostled with my siblings
into the pen—then all at once,
those ears, those eyes

pried upon my youngest brother,
four years old and dawdling
up at tree limbs.

They snapped at his hip,
his shirt, and pulled him
beneath their nose.

I grabbed my brother up—
his body against mine,
mine against fencing,

fencing against the wolves,
the wolves against
a frothing sky above us.

The Lives of Chickens

when they flap out
to scrape the dirt for bugs
        Mom laughs she says
to the chicken with no neck

poor Rhonda no animal will eat you
not without a neck and yet
later we find Rhonda
a popped balloon

a torn cluster of feathers
scattered
over the purple lamps
of bull thistle

        \\

new chicks arrive in the mail
under heat lamps
they smell of mildew shit

every night Mom
sings to them
a chair next to their cage

their eyes fall first
then heads onto other
bodies

        \\

this madness in the barnyard

a rooster
        named *Joy*
but now furious at perhaps
        his name that in no way
        reflects him
terrible as ever
        to my youngest brother
        my sister laughing
pointing at him
        look out!

and there flurried upon
        the lurch of flightless
        feathers Joy
riles head-down toward my brother
        kicking up talons
        earth to earth
skin split open as my brother
        darts between
        barns for shelter
but then curls his fingers
        around an edge to see
        if the phantom has left

but indeed he hasn't
        as the rooster spies
        two hands
that so resemble
        forefathers' hands
        murderers yes
and so claws vengeance upon
        my brother's pink body

　　　　　　for what guilt
can be riffled out

until one day we peel open
　　　　　　the coop door
　　　　　　to find
in the sawdust Joy
　　　　　　his blood sputtered
　　　　　　to silence
beak half open
　　　　　　curved into light
　　　　　　half like
a sickle's point

　　　　　\\

a chicken costs 35 cents

　　　　\\

a possum gnaws wire into the coop

　　　　　　　　eats the foot off
　　　　　　　　Dorothy

Mom lets blood puddle
in her lap

　　　　　　she wraps the stump

maneuvering her hands

> around the remaining
> toe

when the vet arrives
he says

> *I've never done foot reconstruction*
> *for a chicken*

Mom says *do it*

the hen with her new
> foot

> holds down earthworms
> to pluck them apart

\\

at dusk the chickens
in a trance
follow each other

into their coop
as if entering an ark
for the night

Cheers

Gift boxes in our left hands.
In our right, lead ropes,
tethered to our llamas' heads.
Umbilical cords.
How the church fixates
when my family enters
from a side door, draped in
purple bed sheets,
shuffling our clumsy bodies
to a straw-laden manger.
The parishioners chuckle,
their hearts swollen as candles
in a dimly lit rectory, wowing
as the llamas hum,
a response to their carols.
So cute, they think,
these creatures should be
clothed in satin blankets,
tassels and plastic gems
hot-glued to halters.
We stand in the singing
for thirty minutes.
The llamas widen their legs, tithe—
a ritual to be gathered up.

The Leaning Barn

Inside, animals make harbor
among the dirt floor, ebbed into rafters,
into clusters of rusted machinery.

An owl, a fox, a copperhead—
they navigate distances and emptiness
as a strand of horizon without clouds.

Season by season, the barn's walls
have held their angle, onto the metal gate
leaned against a post pile for storage,

some form of pillar. Dad says,
Don't go in there. It could collapse
with a single shifting.

And so, my siblings and I chuck rocks
at the walls, pelting grayed hay stacks
sprouted with grass,

an emerald glow wherever sunlight lands.
We test the roof, ourselves beneath it
for seconds at first, then minutes—

until comfortable to linger, we discover
the bones of an entire cow,
gleaming dirty-white from a lumpy

blanket of dirt. A sculpture and
the discarded fragments of a sculpture.
Horseflies circle my sweaty hair,

heavy as years. The field outside waits,
watching the barn's leaning face
disappear.

An Account of a Llama's Death

Zipporah died two days ago. A good llama, she watched over newborn
crias. Guarded the herd at night against coyotes. She was kind even to
the youngest of my siblings. Dad tied her body to the bush hog and
dragged her to a pit beneath the big tree at our property's end, the
family gravesite where all our animals rest. There, he cut the engine and
tussled her into the earth. My siblings and I looked upon her stiffened
bulk, already losing wool. She had outlived many younger than her.
We shoveled dirt to blanket her from winter, while clouds rolled on the
horizon to drag a cold front in.

Sinkhole

A vulture carries in its one body
many bodies,

like this sinkhole in which I find
a long
                shadow,

a cave widening beneath it.

The pit whittles itself, bloomless,
items poured into it:

beer bottles,
                toasters,
oil cans,
                ovens,
box springs,
                a tractor engine,
plow.

Reddened at the edges, it warms
rust into dirt,
                into rock—

a generous act, too polite,
depended upon.

A home upon land,
                a seldom lifted back.

Fleeing, too,
can be a haven.

Did you notice the climbing

                        wings?

Tasting Moonshine

Along a fence line with my cousin, I point into the fields
and say something about gravel that used to run
through the property, a county road for the region.

He hands me a jar. Says he made it himself.
I take a swig and picture the rust of a barn's roof.
Apple flavor, he says.

He takes back the jar and I choke out, *Good*.
In my throat lingers a pillar of heated glassware,
my tongue a sprig of cinnamon, another gesturing animal.

Is numbness the same as comfort? I feel anxious in crowds.
There's a crowd in me that wants out, wants goddamn air.
Then, I remember: I am along a fence line with my cousin,

talking about the past, as if the past is a godly thing.
It's not. And maybe what I hold in my empty palms
is sacred.

Spit

I hold to it, this spittle,
some pinched web,
thinking how many times

it has glossed a wound,
scrape, burn.
Healing is another word

for work, and work
isn't procedure,
not always.

What tether to life
has a substance?
To ingest is to bury.

\\

In the fields, I consider
the tallest llama,
Moose,

grown antler-high.
As a cria, he drained
his birth mother,

then nursed from one
whose cria, stillborn,
would not suckle.

Now he unlatches
feed bins, the doorknob

to our storage barn.

Click.

The herd plumps up,
despite our shouting,
my family assuming

we alone keep nourishment.

\\

There could be creation
here, without hands,
without something forced.

Even in this farmland,
the calling of it, *farmland*
notes an imposed purpose.

My family builds comfort
around loneliness,
says of this farm,

Peaceful is enough.

\\

Christ, some believe,
shared from his lips
a holiness,

that he asked from soil
a muddy lump,
spat, then pressed

that blessing
into another's eyes.
All the body.

Maybe llamas blossom
a healing,
a seeing beyond

my human frame,
this slow root.
Blood, too,

is a kind of home.
Every time I
cut my lip, I drip

of sunset.
I aim to earth
a tiny downpour.

\\

Outside, I wander
for what—silence?
I blame the hills,

thwacking leaves
off tree limbs, clearing

brush for a pathway.

Look at the violence.
Think of the storm, the teeth.
But really, it's me.

In a rejected gospel,
Jesus compares
his disciples to

small children
living in a field
which isn't theirs.

I remember the llamas.

II.

Mom Woke to a Coyote Staring in Her Window

And now I hear the pack, wayward, yipping
along the fences, the llamas' pastures.

I hurl myself with my siblings
down a long string of gravel into darkness

without a weapon, only our yelling.
We tumble our arms into air,

scoop sticks, hammer an empty oil drum
—every action hawkish, frantic

to prevent dimpled limbs, flustered wool,
bellies hooked open like grain bags.

Meanwhile in the fields, the llamas shape
themselves a circle, siloing their young.

The clamoring flinches, then recedes,
the shadows of knee-high shoulders

turning the hills into blurred absence,
a silence climbed into substance.

Tonight, each living creature becomes
an almanac in mud, having pressed

their pads into the earth and the earth
having embraced them.

Wheatgrass empties in wind, stems
leaning and rising, a rhythm of lungs.

Does everything wail like a body?

Somewhere, the coyotes
untangle their teeth from tendons,

warming themselves
with the displaced light of others.

Myself, a Barbed Wire

Early this morning, I wander
into the farther hills and find,
in the farm of my heart, a warmth
peeled back, ventricles open,
a craving untenable, the strings
of arteries wound into bows.
The barbed wire of this clearing
loop-the-loops with wind
into odd sunsets. At night
their points narrow to the moon,
to several planets orbiting
personal stars. And the trees
have become fence posts.
Ore has become wire,
some artifact that once twined
with rocks beneath me.
Evolution equals fate, equals . . .
Some might claim a sameness
of barbs, saying they've been
fashioned to be the same, but I
see how they are distinct
in their line, even though meant to
draw lines, to keep out or in.
In mist, how tiny droplets
cling to the barbs, then exit
when the sunlight comes.

Blood Lungs

A lung brimmed with blood is a shadow
if air can't pass through
to enter new compartments—

which is me, as I slump in a tepid wheelchair,
my eyelids dizzy music notes, dipped
while a nurse measures my bicep
with a slouched rubber hose.
I ask for air, wishing to carry again
the bronze of a llama farm, a turnip sky.

How did I get here? I remember a leg
squared with my chest. Shears buzzing.
Wool tussled in clumps. Like a gunshot,
spit sprang into another mouth.
So much green on everything.

And it's *everything* that teeters between
rage and forgiveness, between the strings
of withheld logic. Two minutes gone,
I wake to a doctor exhaling,
resting away instruments into familiar
walls of being.

How to Pet a Llama

Let him sniff you first. Breathe easy.
Look him in the eyes
as you would your mother.
Don't pat the head.
He doesn't take being treated
like a dog. Keep your hand
at the neck, your palm down,
as if smoothing out
wrinkled linen. Let your words
slowly out like twine,
like pulling colors from a sleeve,
like a sharing of troubled history.
Llamas carry conversations
as if seated in a rowboat
before fog has lifted, as if pausing
to hear the long echo after
a good shout. Welcome him.
Tenderly, a llama hums—not as if
recalling the tune to a song,
but something longer lost.
Call it a lullaby if you like.
Stand, just the two of you.
Let your breath mingle
as in cold, the air on tiptoe.

Taking in the Stray

The day I found you in the barn, wandered from home or orphaned,
you had so many ticks you lost your sight from blood loss. As you
regained your eyes, I helped you find your way about the house—this
place my family welcomed you and you could call your own. And you
certainly did. The way you sprawled on couches. The way you consumed
rabbits and breezed inside to vomit them on carpet. The way you ate
field mice with their tails writhing, noodles through your teeth. And the
time you brought home a deer limb, crossing the cattle guard to tear its
flesh in front of the llamas as they looked around to see if one of them
had misplaced a leg. You devoured so many sinless creatures. Yet, I still
remember the time you curled beside a fawn to guard it from coyotes.
After you had eaten its mother.

Taking Care

A man in frayed overalls
lost his house to fire last week,
and now his family wades

between the couches
of friends.
Two, three children.

And yet, he has refused
my family's help,
instead has arrived

with our neighbor
to help *us*.
We build a small fence

to keep our dogs in,
so they don't go sniffing out
to where rain has made

the pond swell, where fish
blister and flap, wary-eyed,
in a basin of run-off.

Because dogs love to end
suffering with just a little more,
they would come back

wearing parched blood
and scales on their coats,
apple skins

—O that dying smell.
You could see plainly
how the fish had been

torn without reverence,
how our dogs had taken
sorrow and made it

their joy
—which on some level,
the man in overalls must be

trying to do,
parsing the earth
with each fence post,

his hands
lowering and lifting,
lowering and lifting.

Lyme

Every ending begins with a field.

\\

Mom stems her fingers
with cigarettes, says the smoke
clears a pathway for her lungs.
Breathing has become
a sport for her. *Eight years*, she says,
and wipes her face,
adjusts her tubing to undo a kink.
How a tick has pierced my family.
With that bright red ring,
set flames around our farmhouse.
Blood, a whisper of bruises.

My family, for years, thought *doing*
began with seeing a culprit,
those tiny eyes. And finally,
when the doctors did name the cause,
I rejoiced, oddly,
as if towering wheatgrass
had somehow parted, a doorway
from the suffering temple.

\\

No, just another wall—
and outside, the tide creeps near.
In the hospital again, Mom
speaks in an altered voice,
an accent not her own.

Must be the brain. Must be a feasting.
We must keep her, the doctors say,
learning again how to perform
the most eloquent of drugs,
waves moving,

                claiming.

    \\

Again, the coats. No food.
Screening
then looking at screens.
See the infection. See it.

It sloshes away, a ravenous
puddle expanding, taking with it
sand, grain, flesh—an ocean
quickly then
another ocean.

    \\

O what ladder down is the body.
This time, respiratory failure.
Not the oxygen tank, Mom says.
That's how they hook you.
Her blankets smell of smoke.
Beyond her window, there's a fire
unattended.

    \\

It doesn't end, this disease.

When the meds reach
their location, cells fester
and spill through organs,
another round.

Mom gets dizzy from the leaving,
the tick that's become her.

Does a blood-yoked animal ever
sicken, tune to a pulsing
and wonder
if in blood
it's not blood,
but where the blood goes?

\\

Forlorn. The wicked oars
become anchors.

Silent Treatment

Something has failed,
too easily severed,
   thin as onionskin;

I can't say what,

though I've seen
   my mother's head,

something inside it heaving
her teeth
down.

While my siblings and I
   fork sticks through the
   woods,

  she drifts

between rooms, dusting
furniture,

   the decorative
   artifacts
   of our lives.

She teases
   insects from
windowsills
piles trash bags

   on the doorstep.

Feathers of dog hair lilt
        between grass stalks
        and maybe a
        gust will

                free them.

When the dinner bell
sounds,

Dad pauses in the barnyard,

the rakes
        and buckets

squared into their
places.

On the Fellowship of Rabies

Enormous the sick bat, writhing over leaves,
its body tinfoil, eyes rising.

I remember those eyes, even now.

One of my brothers, three years at the time,
toddled to it and lifted it by a wingtip.

When Mom saw his extended arm from afar,
his bitten knuckles, she cried for him to drop

the pitiful creature. Nothing ever dies simply.
My sister gathered a shovel. Dad boxed it,

drove it to a lab, the eternity of science.
Our brother, shot with a long needle, became

the youngest in Kentucky with a rabies vaccine.
The neighbor has been giving him

high-fives ever since. And today, after we
comfort a dying llama, gums pale

and head thrust into air, we shall each
receive the same vaccine,

a disease carried among us,
a simple leaning of water and drink,

      the brain
          into brain
              into heart.

Climates

mornings my siblings and I scoop shit
we lift pebbles plumping up a wheelbarrow in rain in wind

in frost the pebbles harden we scrape them apart we dump
the pile into our garden the llamas enter

                                         bend

                                             fart

they tithe for the harvest then we scoop it up we carve
the bottoms of our boots with sticks

     \\

hills into two parts a landscape remakes itself
water over sandstone

       ash over fire

            leaf over soil

                 tree over root

                 root

a carving made sculpture

a language made

     \\

            today Mom twirls her dress
            she is wearing a dress
            Dad a tie

            what a lover has
            of the loved the loved
            a lover

            they exit

\\

the neighbor's wolves have dug from their fences
entered into a place of berry and sticker bush
local and more local

a month ago I heard of the female
how a farmer had needled his gun barrel into a cows' field

and shot a horror into her

   \\

Mom drags Dad's table saw into rain it rusts
and cannot bruise even wood it sits in the barn
broken and ignored

   \\

bulbs of onion grass when pulled from earth reveal
pock marks upon soil

which have like loneliness
a note
            of something
                         missing

   \\

the walls of my family's farmhouse

swell in heat
cracks grow back tightly
from winter

        a field mouse
        in the living room

        in the living room
        a cat

a broom stick
draws down

   \\

farm machinery lowers an imprint in soil
what's left of its surface

has washed off
like baptismal oil

   \\

locusts emerge from dirt and I receive
their song their bite marks they don't even notice
how branches have waned

it storms for years upon the hillside

steel towers hold water their shells

                marked with
                paint

\\

Dad arrives home I wake he's at the table he smiles
offers me eggs

I eat he smiles

he teaches me driving says *get in the driver's seat*
I say
hooray

he leans to watch my speedometer says *don't grip*
the steering wheel not so hard
easy

when merging he says *count*
each second
let it each second become a step to
the other
side

\\

Mom cries
for no apparent reason

she has surrounded herself with dogs
tiny dogs
they sleep under blankets their coats too thin for winter

I hug her and cannot see her eyes
but for a moment

her smile

I smile

  \\

because of what could puncture

       branches
       deep-red thorns
       the beak
       of a snapping turtle

I never walk barefoot
  I cover my toes with wool

    then wool
    with rubber
      then rubber
    with mud

  \\

my sister says of the llamas
hers is best
    and my brothers laugh at her

for in a field her llama steals from others
grain bowls emptied
      overturned
       hay in sparse clumps

\\

I too
have etched
toward freedom

        a clean existence

the earth is a film
of dust

        and I think maybe

I could notch glee into it

        wash the dirty surfaces
        over and over

I carve
a smiling face
from dust

        the car's back window
        shimmers

my picture

        through a long-lit
        tunnel

\\

my parents wake me with their arguing
the landscape with their words

a pillow to my ears
        buttons my door shut

Bottom Land

Standing in a murky creek,
I feel the fish nibble
my leg hairs.

I submerge my head
and the dogs look around
as if I've left.

It's No Good

Today, Mom has papers.
She hands them
to Dad,
but Dad will not
take them.
She hugs her papers,
smiles.
Now,
flutters them above
her head.
Now,
spins on her toes.
In another hand,
she has a pen.
Claims it has magic.
Claims her pen
can meet her papers.
Yes,
and if they wish it,
if they wish to cozy up,
they could kiss.
O how she wishes it!
She lays out
each page,
scoots them
together.
Adjusts her pen.
Nods to them,
bows to them—
her new dark
shrine.

Brush Fire

At night, I burn the brush
cut for fruit trees,
my lighter kissed to grass tufts,
the higher branches
tipped with smoke.

I stamp my boots into
the blackened wood, hissing of life,
and the cracking stems
beneath my heels mirror
deer bones between dogs' paws.

When I finish, I spread
the burning embers with a stick;
they look
like constellations.

At the Storm Cellar

When something exists,
there exists an option.
A town away, a man ended

his religion with a gunshot.
The crows will no longer
visit that yard.

Like the crows, I wish to visit
some landless landscape,
perhaps to compare, to try out

a different worship.
I have aged enough to get away.
Although, I will miss

even this storm cellar,
where during Prohibition
the former owner took payment

every other month to store
the bootleggers' bottles.
Where liquor waited

quietly through winter,
the times in which so many found
rebellion in malt grain.

It never smelled of whiskey though,
despite the broken glass.
Perhaps the stones, years ago,

embraced the smell,
the earth returned to earth perhaps,
same as me, as I played

hide-and-seek with my siblings.
Another hour. Maybe everything
will return to its comfortable fashion,

this farm and its histories—
my family too, as we pass
into separation.

I've become perched in memory,
a bootlegger and farmer,
giving and given a choice between

what's present and missing,
while at this doorway and looking
into the mildew darkness.

A car idles in gravel,
its headlights
touching an empty field.

III.

The Afterlife

You'd imagine everything
would be emeralds or perfume,
give it time.
Goodness is this apartment,
these furnishings,
carpet threads cloud-like
except for footprints.
Goodness is this city
where this week I wandered
to a corner, shouted
at the starless sky
and bundled a map
from those next to me.
Is it beauty or betrayal
that I should embrace a crowd
and not the earth?
That I can stroll to the porches
of friendship
and be just as happy?
How good it is,
goodness everywhere.

Tussle

an irony that a city too
wishes to be among a farm

    and the highway sides
    nudge openly with weeds

how flower boxes
tend doorways and sills

    how gardeners shape bushes
    into absent animals

is a fountain mimicry

    is landscaping devotion
    a practice at religion

the awnings of branches
fill up with new air

    people feast upon mulch

and what are landmarks
without passage

    what are holes in gutters
    if not light upon wounds

it all drips into puddles
gently arranged rocks

to decorate a void
to accompany a life

a without and so

a farm equals a city
a city a farm

one spiraling blur
one wilderness

an against and with

a window
and what beyond it

Leaving the Farm

I've dropped my roots
on concrete slabs.
No mud here.

Here they call it filth.
And I am a city boy inside
the body of a country.

My youth speaks a language
of disconnected noise.
Who travels a decade

without collecting scars?
I've cut my hands,
made them hard

on hay bale strings.
And I've seen wheat,
copper in sunset, balled on the hills.

I've seen hope lift and bob in wind,
a landscape not of metal,
the only towers, silos.

Here hovers a different moon,
dotted with the firecrackers
of gunshots and horn honks.

How I miss the fields sometimes.
I regret that I've become
a person forgotten of silence.

I'm trying to find grace
in the sternness of a parking meter,
in crumbling sidewalk squares.

Endings can be
what the lesser gods call *good*,
but I'm okay if a farm's ending

waits a little while.
At night, train horns share
no whereabouts.

Sunlight paints the body
of a lamppost
same as any fence slat,

even though one surface
rests level, the other
rounded.

Portrait of Truth as a Satisfied Belly

maybe this is the way of it
an appearing without coaxing
a nest that sprouts
from an open mailbox

to crack an egg means
to will an inside out
to unwind a shell as feathers do

a feather warms
rather than be warmed
an egg is an early feather
a pause for what path

an animal from dark
has rummaged into the box
eaten the eggs
beads of yolk dapple the soil

Evolution Chart

I shake my hands over a sink like my great-aunts did,
two women who lived together
among perched tobacco, sliced halves of fruit,
jaundiced tabloids, sharing with me
handfuls of candy, blue and red chocolate beads,
while plucking out their favorites,
the green ones, and holding them up, between
their thumbs and index fingers, dimes just high enough,
so that the light of porch windows offered the cocoa shells
a good melting. Their house had been a schoolhouse
a century ago, its bell still there, the yard a yard for play,
then a backyard, one land. How things do linger.
When I was a child on my father's shoulders,
I'd touch my hands to a ceiling and call it
my second floor. To travel your childhood means
never to age. Watch. I am attempting as far back
as time will take me. Already, I am somewhere else.
I hold my hands to a towel, cover them,
the surface like fur, and I think maybe this feeling
recalls some earlier animal.

Everywhere the Salt

A body
in affection loosens.

Does anyone know
the number of years that *love*

has moved humans
—millions?

My neighbor would lower
upon his wife's grave

two flowers each day.
Since fourth grade,

he'd etched her name
to folded notebook paper,

swung jubilant from the limbs
of summer, that kindly air.

The cemetery's ground
softened to his footprints.

He welcomed it.

By the time the living turned over
his down-faced mound,

vultures had already seen his body,
thought from their branches,

surely, they'd been
blessed.

The Way Home

I look into an amber-necked bottle
and remember the route
as a calligraphy of tree branches,
the winter's bone-filling wet.
From our family van, I would see
the power company's bulbless
walls, a lineage of wires,
the elderly draft horse, his head
lowered over grass clumps,
so many abandoned threshers
and round bales wrapped too tight
like plaster. Homesickness can howl
a kind of guilt, as I am guilty
to think a place my own.
Every land begets and receives
a trauma: dynamite-blasted
highways, flint shards in creek beds,
smoke where animals
flee upon burning paws.
I take sips to open my mouth,
but my ears, my ears.

IV.

Breakage

When my parents' divorce
punctured my family,
Mom had tried to keep the herd,
tried anything
to have their happiness be
her happiness too.

A truck jostled down our driveway,
creaking with a long trailer
and rust flaking off
onto the gravel rock.

When the llamas entered into that
enclosure, their groups
of six each trip,
spread over sixteen months,
I lived elsewhere,
visiting on occasion,

trying to separate myself
from myself,
a numbing to all things
loved and loving.

I never said goodbye
to any llama, never asked
when the trailer arrived
if tails swatted at the cool air,
if eyes flickered upon
our pastures shrinking behind hills,

if seeds clung hard
to matted coats and traveled
as companion to that new
uneven somewhere.

Inadequate Prayers

Maybe they dither at cloudy gates,
clogged between bars,

lounged about at the feet
of St. Peter, who kicks them

from his path; or
still on earth, forgotten,

wandering valleys and rooftops.
Maybe they have been

sheltered for years into closets,
attics, basements.

In the slivers of concrete
where weeds throw up tired arms,

in the emptying pockets
of donated jeans or stirring

the silence inside geodes, grain silos,
junkyard car engines.

And on my lips too.
I am releasing one just now,

letting it loose without hope
into air. The way a surface

welcomes moss,
a hill with overgrowth.

And see the masonry stones
of an unbuilt home,

piled
then abandoned.

Say each placement equals
a hand,

each hand a togetherness,
the way hands move,

piling then letting
stones tilt.

It could be a kind of god,
this untouched thing.

A meaning in not having
meaning, a void.

O little prayers that go
and go nowhere,

uttered for sake of utterance.

Still, why is anything
a fortress.

Final Visit

The whole place has become cicada shells,
weakened at the walls, the door frames,
the yellowed ceiling in the living room
with its crack, spread now a little larger.
The bird dish has broken into three pieces.
The propane tank lowers with its fumes.
Even the weeds have been flurried
with the wet film of frost.

Is this what endings look like?

    \\

Down at the barn, three of the llamas
remain; the others having gone
away into the reaches of countryside,
to a woman I've just learned
is also getting a divorce.
Even these three, as they pass through
the gates left open,
will go upriver soon. They will
nibble on hay and grain and, if not,
be fed to dogs.

    \\

Like the gray fox
found in the neighbor's barn
years ago, its eyes and coat
closed of reason and wrapped in secrecy,
what's rare has become
synonymous with extinction.

Vultures needle their toes
around the silo's brim.
Let mercy be what guides us.

\\

Around eight degrees
and a chicken has gone missing.
I go down to the coop, stroll every field.
How fitting that I should be
searching for something in darkness.
I scour my flashlight into low branches
of thorny trees, as if the hen perches up there,
a patron saint of winter, looking down at me.

I return to the house and tell my mom something
must've eaten it—though no feathers,
so maybe, by luck,
it'll turn up by morning.

\\

I explore the hills unknowable as a graveyard
what future they'll have.
The creeks and ponds swell up
and harden over like welts,
where even the pine trees
bow in the wind like bodies.

Nothing Is Clean in the Country

After my family sold the farm,
Mom wouldn't leave.
Delayed the trucks. Had to take
the kitchen cabinets too.

They're going to make our home
a hunting lodge, she said.
They're going to blow apart
those poor forest animals.

The rich couple couldn't afford
patience. They knew the governor,
an easy phone call.
When they evicted Mom,

it was a locked door,
a handwritten note. She left
at dark without boxes.
The next day, they called back

the police. Said from cameras,
they could tell my youngest brother
was still there, come quick . . .
but a groundskeeper raised open

his dusty palms.
He'd been fixing light bulbs,
tossing furniture into dumpsters,
converting one ownership

into another. What does it mean
to settle from a hundred acres

into one? In a flowerpot suburb,
my youngest brother

walks a stretch of asphalt daily,
no stick in hand, no trees
around him. The neighbors
have decided fences take

from space a kind of power.
But the rabbits don't care.
They enter onto lawns
thinking, *O what a feast.*

Monochromatic Untethering

The fragments of a life, carried in full arms. Lay the pieces
out into a pretty line, set them into daylight,

a yearning. Those days and every day. I understand now
the nature of cliché, a welcomed easiness, a mantra

—but anything said often hasn't meaning anymore, has become
thrummed string echoed across canyons as large as ribs.

Imagine jumping into a tall river, the molecules
collecting around you so wildly, so familiar.

I am trying to name what it is, this formidable want
for belonging and safety—and I am woven with howling,

myself so shaped by wool, a sweater removed, my hair
in a static eruption. When the lights go out, blue.

End of the Llamas

let llamas give freely of their wool
a gift of spreading   those two L's

enough to crawl through   like into a sky
without beliefs

we share what we share   and in sharing
our sometimes spit   sometimes anger

grin-less grins of joy   we also share
a soil   by god   on which to walk

mud caked and stickers   like little children
where if to plant feet

means to make a home

     \\

a llama bounds from the toe
down a length of pasture   ears up

nosing the wind like   *huzzah!*
O sweet llama   my llama

in a field of llamas
now not in a field   or are you

I remember that lovely wonder
have wondered if I could

match that joy   sing

through my teeth   lips closed

head to the earth   a mouth
of clover and seed

llama   what about the world

you are TV show   children's book
zoo exhibit   coffee mug

how is it then   the use
of presence

when I held lead rope   I held
a magic in my palm

and now   I am no longer farmer

unnamed

          unnamed

          \\

llamas return again to my windows
and I follow them

O what deep   eternal bucket
I might lean into

brimming   touched by tongues
          no

wake up   wake up

the llamas are gone

maybe my body is now the farm
a housing   where now I

carry them
        carry them

      \\

in the gaunt buildings
of small talk   llamas would perch

upon my handshakes   a mention
without mention

of family   my inward tumult

I would seat upon the warm
glamor of llamas   to avoid

what questions might froth
to air   hovering without answers

how fare the llamas   what of
your family   what for

I swallowed them down
okay with a name   a name like

llama guy   every fountain
enough to drink

to say the whole
meant to regret   so I apportioned myself

      with comfort

but in a portion   another portion
reaches

what map could the earth be   what gift
of looking in

inside my gut   my parents' divorce
inflates   pops

like a pool tube   I crimp the sides
the rubbery definition

to cleave   to dissolve   to expel
out
     out

   \\

I have tried goodbye
a hundred times   why then

do I feel
my tongue hasn't moved

\\

I imagine how the pastures have mended
the mud grown wild

into green   so much of what couldn't
sprout beforehand

I become   at this edge
a pain   a healing

a throat from silence
a strange willingness   as if what's left

why shouldn't I
encourage all of it gone

The Light and Where It Lives

Disheveled seeds upon soil,
wriggling, survived—
anything lost is anything

to gain in emptiness.
I wish enough,
to have only

these memories I have.
Yes. This too is a prayer,
an opening palm.

I never was any good at farming,
always wanting for the city,
the luxury of a shorter walk.

I would see a speckled beetle
hobbling in grass and be
reminded of solitude.

Now that I live in a city,
something about community
tends a community in me.

Because the farmer's market on Market
is only what it is
and what I carry.

Because on 54th a meal
fits upon a table
simply as a menu.

Because this city has become
an embrace I prefer
and yes, what could grow does,

this heft of sweetness,
this quiet bag of grain that widens
with new harvest.

Praise be. Praise be
the forums of communion,
found anywhere if sought.

Before, I had only wanted for
another day, all while not
seeing every person,

the privilege I had,
not waking during night
to car lights, sirens, hunger.

I've climbed from being
of dirt, rough fingernails,
and I still don't know

the purpose of dirt.
When I drive the long route
between this city, that city;

I notice the weeds
with newer eyes, how they
lift beyond fence wire.

Finishing the Harvest

I remember hoisting bales up to a hay wagon,
thud by thud into a stack seven blocks high,
piling them into a barn and spacing them
foot-wide, so Kentucky wouldn't swelter the loft into flame.
And maybe oak branches, unable to touch the earth,
do envy the stems freed from their soil, split apart
and swimming into stomachs as livestock, wildlife, wind
will churn a finished harvest into one of their own.
Even pain can have an outward-traveling happiness,
a happiness like the kind you will find
in the passenger pickup lane at airports,
how people throw their jubilance out,
tossing it around bodies, saying *Hello* or *Welcome.*
Watch the luggage straps, how they lift and place
with such an ease. Something you can let go,
when ready, from your fingers like joy.

The Lesser Distances

Mom lifts a coffee, joy by the brim. On her wall, a painting of the farm. Pictures of her children. In her body, freedom. In Dad's body, freedom and a little more belly. Across town, he steers a boat down a river to another river. It's a blessing, this healing. I visit between their couches, tidying clothes in a suitcase. In winter, we drink eggnog. Bourbon. Pull cookies from heat and eat them. The Christmas trees shed their bristles, slowly with a kind of forgiveness. Stockings on hooks with new names.

Notes

"Spit" references the Gospel of Thomas in the lines "*small children / living in a field / which isn't theirs*"; the passage appears in *The Gnostic Gospels* by Alan Jacobs (London: Watkins, 2006). There's also a reference to John 9:6–7 earlier in the poem.

The poems in this collection comprise a fictionalized version of the poet's life.

Acknowledgments

My deepest gratitude to the following publications where poems from this book first appeared, many in earlier versions:

Barely South Review: "Myself, a Barbed Wire"
Birmingham Poetry Review: "Breakage," "Evolution Chart," "Inadequate Prayers"
Colorado Review: "Portrait of Truth as a Satisfied Belly"
Court Green: "Tasting Moonshine"
Geometry: "Bottom Land"
Grist: "The Way Home"
Hotel Amerika: "Taking in the Stray"
Los Angeles Review: "Lyme"
The Minnesota Review: "Laws of Motion," "Mom Woke to a Coyote Staring in Her Window"
Notre Dame Review: "The Lives of Chickens"
Permafrost: "The Leaning Barn"
The Pinch: "Final Visit"
Prairie Schooner: "End of the Llamas," "Nothing Is Clean in the Country," "Silent Treatment"
Puerto del Sol: "Tussle"
River Styx: "How to Pet a Llama"
Sequestrum: "Brush Fire"
Sixfold: "The Llama Named 'James and John Sons of Thunder'" (as "We Have a Llama Whose Name Is 'James and John Sons of Thunder'"), "An Account of a Llama's Death"
Slice Magazine: "Taking Care"
Southern Humanities Review: "Sinkhole"
Sugared Water: "Leaving the Farm"
Tahoma Literary Review: "Finishing the Harvest"

Yemassee: "Blood Lungs"

"The Llama Named 'James and John Sons of Thunder'" (as "We Have a Llama Whose Name Is 'James and John Sons of Thunder'") and "An Account of a Llama's Death" also appeared in *New Poetry from the Midwest 2014* (New American Press, 2015).

"Brush Fire" was a runner-up of *Sequestrum*'s 2016 New Writer Awards.

I would like to warmly thank everyone who offered their friendship, feedback, and encouragement over the years when I was composing these poems, including John Sibley Williams, Noah Davis, Todd Davis, Conor Bracken, Michael Baumann, Aaron Wilder, Luke S., Kelli Prejean, Anna Rollins, Laura Sonderman, Haley Fedor, Angie Mazakis, Joel Peckham, Darius Atefat-Peckham, Kevin Carollo, Nayt Rundquist, Travis Dolence, Bob Vivian, Cody Lumpkin, Adam Vines, Neil Carpathios, Amelia Martens, Charlotte Pence, and most especially my poetry teachers A.E. Stringer, Rachael Peckham, and David Shumate.

A monumental thanks to Anita Skeen, Laurie Hollinger, and the RCAH Center for Poetry; and to Amanda Frost, Kristine Blakeslee, Elise Jajuga, Gennie Martin, Julie Loehr, and the entire Michigan State University Press team for bringing this book into the world.

Eternal gratitude to Gabrielle Calvocoressi for believing in this book, for giving it a home. It is an honor beyond words.

Thank you to all my past teachers in Kentucky, Indiana, and West Virginia.

Special thanks to the English Department at Marshall University, to all the friends I made there.

Additional thanks and honor to my old Kentucky neighbors, including farther down the road, Wendell Berry.

A huge, boisterous thank you to my enormous family, living in Kentucky and elsewhere, particularly to Mom, Dad, Austin, William, Mary, and Michael—I love you all. When I'm with you, I feel at home.

Lastly, to my wife, Rebecca, and my children, Benjamin and Clara: I love each of you so deeply. Of this world, I cherish you most—what a beautiful place, with you in it.

SERIES ACKNOWLEDGMENTS

We at Wheelbarrow Books have many people to thank without whom Daniel Lassell's *Spit* would never be in your hands. We begin by thanking all those writers who submitted manuscripts to the eighth Wheelbarrow Books Prize for Poetry. We want to single out the finalists: Benjamin Gucciardi, *West Portal*; Ceridwen Hall, *Acoustic Shadows*; Anne Haven McDowell, *Breath on a Coal*; and Mitchell Nobis, *We Hold These Truths*, whose manuscripts moved and delighted us and which we passed on to the final judge, along with Daniel Lassell's manuscript, for her reading. That judge, Gabrielle Calvocoressi, we thank for her thoughtful selection of the winner and her critical comments offered earlier in this book.

Our thanks to assistant to the director, Estee Schlenner, and Center for Poetry interns Lydia Barron, Jillian Bowe, Jayla Harris-Hardy, Charlotte Krause, Kaylee McCarthy, and Fabrizzio Torero for their careful reading of manuscripts and insightful commentary on their selections, and especially to Laurie Hollinger, acting director at the RCAH Center for Poetry, who also read the manuscripts and provided the logistical aid and financial wizardry for this project. Sarah Teppen, a previous RCAH Center for Poetry intern, designed our Wheelbarrow Books logo which makes us smile every time we see it.

We also thank Stephen Esquith, dean of the Residential College in the Arts and Humanities, who has given his continued support to the RCAH Center for Poetry and Wheelbarrow Books since our inception. As we began thinking seriously about Wheelbarrow Books, conversation with June Youatt, then provost at Michigan State University, was encouraging and MSU Press director Gabriel Dotto and assistant director/editor-in-chief Julie Loehr were eager to support the efforts of poets to reach a hungry audience. We cannot thank them enough for having faith in us, and a love of literature, to collaborate on this project.

Thanks to our current editorial board, Sarah Bagby, Gabrielle Calvocoressi, Leila Chatti, Mark Doty, George Ellenbogen, Carolyn Forché, Thomas Lynch, George Ella Lyon, and Naomi Shihab Nye for believing Wheelbarrow Books a worthy undertaking and lending their support and their time to our success.

Finally, to our patrons: without your belief in the Wheelbarrow Books Poetry Series and your generous financial backing we would still be sitting around the conference table adding up our loose change. You are making it possible for poets who have never had a book of poetry published, something that's becoming harder and harder these days with so many presses discontinuing their publishing of poetry, to find an outlet for their work. You are also supporting the efforts of established poets to continue to reach a large and grateful audience. We name you here with great admiration and appreciation:

Beth Alexander   Patricia and Robert Miller
Mary Hayden   Brian Teppen
Jean Kruger

WHEELBARROW BOOKS

Anita Skeen, *Series Editor*

Sarah Bagby   Carolyn Forché
Mark Doty   Thomas Lynch
George Ellenbogen   Naomi Shihab Nye

Wheelbarrow Books, established in 2016, is an imprint of the RCAH Center for Poetry at Michigan State University, published and distributed by MSU Press. The biannual Wheelbarrow Books Poetry Prize is awarded every year to one emerging poet who has not yet published a first book and to one established poet.

SERIES EDITOR: Anita Skeen, professor in the Residential College in the Arts and Humanities (RCAH) at Michigan State University, founder and past director of the RCAH Center for Poetry, director of the Creative Arts Festival at Ghost Ranch, and director of the Fall Writing Festival.

The RCAH Center for Poetry opened in the fall of 2007 to encourage the reading, writing, and discussion of poetry and to create an awareness of the place and power of poetry in our everyday lives. We think about this in a number of ways, including through readings, performances, community outreach, and workshops. We believe that poetry is and should be fun, accessible, and meaningful. We are building a poetry community in the Greater Lansing area and beyond. Our undertaking of the Wheelbarrow Books Poetry Series is one of the gestures we make to aid in connecting good writers and eager readers beyond our regional boundaries. Information about the RCAH Center for Poetry at MSU can be found at http://poetry.rcah.msu.edu and also at https://centerforpoetry.wordpress.com and on Facebook and Twitter (@CenterForPoetry).

The mission of the Residential College in the Arts and Humanities at Michigan State University is to weave together the passion, imagination, humor, and candor of the arts and humanities to promote individual well-being and the common good. Students, faculty, and community partners in the arts and humanities have the power to focus critical attention on the public issues we face and the opportunities we have to resolve them. The arts and humanities not only give us the pleasure of living in the moment but also the wisdom to make sound judgments and good choices.

The mission, then, is to see things as they are, to hear things as others may, to tell these stories as they should be told, and to contribute to the making of a better world. The Residential College in the Arts and Humanities is built on four cornerstones: world history, art and culture, ethics, and engaged learning. Together they define an open-minded public space within which students, faculty, staff, and community partners can explore today's common problems and create shared moral visions of the future. Discover more about the Residential College in the Arts and Humanities at Michigan State at http://rcah.msu.edu.